MASTER EFFECTIVE TEAM MANAGEMENT

Marcel Boer & Emelia Pillay

Copyright © 2020 Marcel Boer

All rights reserved.

ISBN: 9798640976977

MASTER EFFECTIVE TEAM MANAGEMENT

TABLE OF CONTENTS

1	Introduction	3
2	Start By Making An Adaptive Plan	6
3	Delegate To The Right People	20
4	Establish A Communication Model	32
5	Establish A Collaboration Model	42
6	Conclusion	67
7	References	69
8	About The Authors	72

1 INTRODUCTION

Team management is something subordinates often think of as an easy job. They believe that their manager is always sitting around and has little 'real' work to take care of. Yet, sadly this is not the case, and it's far from the reality.

The role of a manager is, unfortunately, underestimated due to the poor visibility around this role. People don't understand the requirements needed by a team manager, and, sometimes, team managers don't know the criteria themselves. That's all good and well, but you're probably asking - what does this have to do with you?

Perhaps, you're the new team manager on the team. Having been an exemplary individual producer who got results for your organization, you've had a promotion to a higher role. Now, it's your turn to fill the shoes of your manager. You're excited and nervous at the same time. The concept of managing your colleagues seems intimidating. You wonder if they will also gossip about you and if you will be any good at the role.

Hold on for a moment; it may surprise you to find out that many have gone before you and felt the same way. The good news for you is that their vast knowledge has enabled us to compile a step-by-step guide that will take you from a nervous team manager to an effective one that consistently supports, engages and grows their team.

This tool is a guide that we wished that we had when we started our journey as team managers. The reality is that nobody quite prepares you for the vast amounts of challenges waiting on your doorstep. This includes difficulties from recruitment, people management, and delegation.

Let's take a walk through what you can expect in the next four chapters.

We'll start our journey looking at management through the lens of a planner, and we'll equip you with tools to plan for your team and the organization while also maintaining your sense of sanity and calmness. As you know, planning is vital to align the strategy of a business and the operations while ensuring the company keeps on moving forward.

From here, we'll broach the topic of delegating your way to productivity while grooming and mentoring your next layer of management. You will learn how to delegate effectively and still have ample time for growing and engaging your team.

Naturally, delegation will lead you to understanding the ultimate communication model that will take mediocre efforts on your team projects to sterling and incredible game-changing results. And you'll be surprised to find that communication will be one of the critical factors for your success as a team manager.

And the final chapter will introduce you to the fine art of collaborating with everyone in your organization effectively. And we'll leave space for you to see for yourself that collaboration involves high levels of emotional intelligence, a quest for building relationships, and a knack for leveraging your networks and supporting your team to do their best work.

With that said, we're happy to see we have a splendid roadmap to kick off your journey through team management. Let's start by planning for success in the first chapter.

2 START BY MAKING AN ADAPTIVE PLAN

Perhaps you've heard the adage that failing to plan is planning to fail, and you now realize that as you move higher up the ranks in your organization, it's true. Yet, as we mentioned in our introduction, team management is indeed a skill that needs time and attention to learn. And you have to decide what you hope to achieve with this skill.

Many new managers have high hopes of making a difference and inspiring the people they manage. Some are hell-bent on not making the same mistakes that their manager made with their teams. Yet, as with most things, to achieve your goals of being an effective manager, you will need to plan for your success. In this chapter, we discuss the critical factors required for planning effectively as a team manager.

We'll look in-depth at the strategies you can employ to start seeing how you can contribute effectively as a manager. And we'll map out the granular level of detail needed for your plan, the important meetings and responsibilities as well as how to map out the perfect vision and goals in conjunction with your team.

Contents

1. Start with the why
2. Team strategy session
3. Success factors
4. Challenges and solutions
5. The way forward

1. Start with the why

In his now hugely popular talk, Simon Sinek illustrates how good leaders communicate their vision and why people follow these leaders. This talk discusses the golden circle and shows how it's an excellent model for leadership and strategic management. He prompts you to think about why some leaders are more influential than others. And it was found through his extensive research that leaders think and act consistently when using the golden circle.

In this circle, there are three key ideas. Leaders should always have a 'Why,' a 'How,' and a 'What' when communicating a message.

Let's unpack each of these aspects below.

What: This represents the products or services that a company offers and is being communicated. In the case of Apple, their products are vast including iPhones, watches, Macbook's and more.

How: This represents what the company does. Sticking with the Apple example. They let us know that their products are eye-catching and also simple to use.

Why: This is all about what the company believes and what they hope to provide value on. And of course, Apple tells us that they think differently and challenge the status quo.

Therefore, always start with the 'Why' when communicating a message. Many managers communicate the 'What' first, and quickly this loses most team members as the 'What' is more tangible and less inspirational.

The aim is to start with the 'Why' first. People are more interested in why you do what you do. As a manager, begin with reasons for your team's roles and cultivate what success looks like for your organization.

How do you do this?

As a starting point, your team will need you to take the lead in defining their ultimate goal as a team. For example, if your team operates in the customer experience sector, the goal may be to improve the customer service rating for your organization from an 8 to a 9.5 out of 10.

Yet, the goal you should realize is only the tangible output. For your team to succeed, you need proper inputs and drivers of performance.

Drivers of team performance

There are three critical drivers of excellent performance for a team that can be incorporated into your plan.

Leadership: Excellent leadership is critical for a successful team and a huge factor when it comes to mediocre teams versus outstanding ones. Leaders are responsible for setting the standard of high performance in an organization. A leader's role is to create, share, and communicate a vision that a team can rally behind.

Taking ownership: This is usually the follow-through mechanism to test if a team is high performing or not. You will see this manifest when you see progress on agreed to actions by your team members.

Either that or the progress is not moving the needle on the project at hand. In high performing teams, people are held accountable and take responsibility for delivering the best work.

Yet every part of your organization must commit to not passing the buck, and soon the culture strengthens its capability.

A pro tip is that employees want to have autonomy, and the best teams are ones that don't need a micromanager. These teams proactively manage you upwards.

Compelling vision: A great team has a compelling vision to get behind, and due to this, it keeps everyone aligned and moving the needle on projects. A compelling vision has all the makings for success, and something everyone in the team can aspire to create.

A compelling vision

The next section will highlight the characteristics of a compelling vision.

Clarity: A clear vision will bring clarity. Since the goal of a vision statement is to guide you and your team to move projects forward, it must be explicit and evident. This ensures that everyone is on the same page at every stage of the work project.

Purpose: A vision with purpose will build authority for you as the team manager; it will give your team a sense of doing meaningful work for your organization. This facet will make driving results that much simpler for you.

Value-driven: Many vision statements are an umbrella term for what an organization stands for. Accompanying a vision is a set of values that everyone on the team commits to. Generally, most teams will follow the organization's larger values and align with their team goals. The core values are the beliefs about good and bad behavior needed for an organization to succeed. In doing so, the value statement will influence employees' attitudes for the work they do.

Vivid and unique: A vision should be convincing and imaginative so much, so when team members see it, they must be able to imagine the future. And it should be unique, and something that makes every team member feel special.

Examples

These are a few examples of compelling visions to spur your inspiration to come up with your own.:

1. "Our vision is to create a better everyday life for many people." - IKEA
2. "Bring inspiration and innovation to every athlete* in the world. (*If you have a body, you are an athlete.)" - Nike
3. "Connect with friends and the world around you." - Facebook

Practical tips

Like with most things, the creation of a compelling vision can be challenging. In our experience, it's the most challenging aspect of getting the team going. A few years back, we were working on a video branding project for our organization, and we organized the best minds to create this video.

The reality is that when the C-suite saw this video, they hated it immensely. The main reason was that there was a poor vision communicated. Due to this, there was a lack of understanding and commitment from the team to the vision.

After reflecting on these challenges, we've come up with four practical tips to ensure you have a compelling team vision below:
1. Be clear about where you're going and make sure you test the clarity with your team members.
2. Go big or go home. This means don't be afraid to think boldly about the future and reach metrics, or goals you believe are possible at that moment.
3. Start with a purpose in mind. Ask why this is important and how it can impact people's lives. And most importantly - why should everyone care about this?
4. Go about setting strategic goals.

You have started with the 'why' and have a compelling, shared vision. It's time to talk about team strategy and tactical ideas to meet your vision

2. Team strategy session

The links between developing a successful team and creating a team strategy is undeniable. There are so many great opportunities when you plan as a team, and this section will show you how to do this.

Steps to take for good team strategy

Step 1: Ensure that your team understands the purpose of strategic planning. The mission, of course, is to design a plan for your business unit to have success in the future. Also, consider the role team members will likely play.

Step 2: You should schedule time to host a strategy meeting where every team member can provide ideas for moving the business unit forward. This meeting can be a brainstorming session or strategic session offsite.

Step 3: Make sure that everyone has a voice, and all notes are recorded so that an action plan for the way forward can be created and distributed.

Step 4: Set the most appropriate timelines for critical aspects during the strategy session and allocate roles for various team members.

Complete these steps, and you will have a working plan that all team members have created together. You will see the results come to fruition as you get buy-in from the team.

The next point of call is to make your vision as visible as possible. You should consider the following activities to ensure that the vision, goal, and strategic team outcomes are always apparent.

Making your vision and strategic objectives visible

We've included four essential tips that will help you and your team write down the key objectives and make it memorable.

1. Create T-shirts for the whole team that shows the vision and strategic objectives.
2. Ensure that all documents include the vision, and this is distributed to all team members.
3. Add this as a reminder for all connect sessions with each team member.
4. Have a monthly strategic meeting where everyone shares their progress.

Let's move onto further aspects of planning that we'll use to create accountability now that we have a vision and team planning enabled.

Schedule weekly check-in sessions
Often meeting with your team is a great way to keep the importance of the vision at the top of mind, yet we get busy and forget to make those checks.

The best idea is to schedule all connect sessions in advance and as a recurring meeting request. As an additional point, you want to have some form of document to distribute so that team members can complete this and send it back to you once a week.

It will aid in keeping people's minds on the goal at hand. Weekly check-in sessions also give you a dipstick check to see how engaged your team is with the vision and strategy the team created.

Do these sessions on a one-on-one basis or as a team session.

You should also consider innovative approaches to connecting, such as the following:

- Having lunch together and catching up on the week, and even listening in on any challenges or misconnection with the vision.

- Random coffee moments with team members with the sole purpose of checking in around their progress.
- A fun game of 30 seconds as an ice breaker before check-ins - it helps with the overall mood in the room.

While many people can hide their actual progress, you will get valuable input on how things are going at present, and you can use this to tweak the management flow of your teams.

3. Success factors

If your planning has gone well, you may notice the following characteristics in your team's performance.

Shared purpose

Usually, when teams are in the starting phase, there is a newfound energy to create and build something unique. This shared common purpose makes people work more and also remain consistently enthusiastic. For example, when we launched a campaign to improve staff sentiment in the management team.

At first, our team members were hesitant. They had just received the results from a staff sentiment survey and were rated quite poorly. Yet, a week later, we held a strategy session to bring the scores up and improve the staff sentiment. And the tone of the room had changed since we brainstormed a goal and vision for the way forward.

Priorities are clear

As a rule of thumb, when team members have a clear idea of what needs to be done, by whom and when then they feel more engaged. It means that at the outset, a worthy goal and vision was set and communicated. You will see this in more open communication and collaboration in the team. There will also be a sense of ownership in each team member.

Roles are adequately defined

There isn't a case of confusion as all team members know the strengths of the team and who is responsible for the various tasks that make the organization run well. It's a great space to be in as not one side will have more work than another, and there will be less animosity that people are not doing the work they need to be doing.

As an example, working with a Customer Relationship Management team can be taxing, as their sole role is to support high-value clients often via e-mail, calls, and other exchanges. Usually, before we had a concrete role definition - the team was not as productive as they needed to be.

Therefore, there was a lot of finger-pointing. Eventually, we held a strategy session focussing on solutions, created a team charter of values, goals, and vision. It worked wonderfully, and we saw improved results.

People feel empowered

There is less micromanaging from your end as the team manager, as everyone knows what they need to do, how to do it, and there is always a feedback loop. They do their work independently and feel proud to be making a decision and contributing positively.

Respect for authority

There is a marked lack of dissent in the team. People understand the rules of engagement for leadership and what's appropriate based on the values agreed to by everyone. In cases where there is a lack of respect for authority, people dissent often and insidiously often roping in other team members, creating an unhealthy and toxic work environment.

Success

Since goals and targets are set out and communicated, it's so easy to measure if the team has been successful, once done, it creates newfound pride in the group as a whole wanting to do even more great things together. And of course, a team that succeeds together grows together. Also, rewards should follow after each team milestone.

A health insurance company we consulted for often held a 'Top Performer Lunch' to celebrate the best teams in the organization. This gesture is a significant motivating factor and made teams feel quite proud of their achievements.

4. Challenges and solutions

As with most great teams, a team manager will always be in the position to observe many challenges along the way, especially in the planning phase.

We've summarised the top challenges managers face during their first six months as a team manager when planning.

Lack of leadership

As a new manager, you often are entirely new on your journey leading and managing people. This point can lead to all sorts of problems such as imposter syndrome, and team members are failing to recognize your authority. Often this lack of influence that they perceive leads to group disregard for all planning efforts. Therefore, they do their own thing.

The problem here is that you have not taken the time to connect authentically with your team and understood their challenges. If you initiated visions and goals without connection, your organization would be unmotivated to follow your lead. They need to know why you do what you do, and they need to feel a sense of connection with you and how you can help them.

Solution: Ensure that you always schedule a connect session with each team member and discuss their goals, success, and also what drives them. Do the same and share information about you so that they can get a sense of what you're like as a person, and this will bring a sense of connection.

Lack of structure

Lack of structure could mean a variety of things. Many times you have not delegated appropriately or organized your team effectively, resulting in utter confusion for everyone.

When teams have a clear goal, direction, and outcome, and they know who is doing what, this problem will go away really quickly. As the manager, you need to diagnose the problem and find methods to resolve the issues swiftly.

Solution: Get to know your team members strengths and understand how you can empower your team members to build the structure of the team together.

Poor resource management

When there is a lack of resources to go around, people will find it challenging to do the work needed, and understandably will not be fully committed to sticking with the plan.

Generally, the organization decides on the resources every year, and the C-suite makes these decisions. Yet, as the manager, your role is to ensure that your team is adequately staffed to prevent burnout. Also, make sure that they have everything they need to do their best work.

Solution: Observe your team in action and how they perform their work. It will open your eyes to the impact of inadequate resources and help you plea for more from the powers that be.

5. The way forward

Our hope in this chapter was to give you a simple, practical approach to plan for your team and the demands associated. As the team manager, you indeed have many demands placed upon you.

But with careful planning, incorporating your team and strategizing on how to make the vision a reality will ensure you succeed at the highest level. It's now up to you to start to implement these tools that will maximize your team's efficiency tenfold.

Here's how you do this and still stay sane:

1. **Create a climate for planning:** Make sure you think about everything you need to plan effectively, such as the resources, people, and setting.
2. **Ask for help from your manager:** Your manager has been there, seen that and understood the challenges. They will be able to help you and mentor you.
3. **Aim to improve every day and communicate effectively:** Communicating well takes practice, and choosing to have a growth mindset. Keep this in mind when it seems like planning is not going your way.

4. **Understand that mistakes help you grow:** Fail forward and do better. If you keep this in mind, your mistakes will make you a better manager over time.

3 DELEGATE TO THE RIGHT PEOPLE

In our last chapter, we tackled the issue of planning, and we touched briefly on delegating work as well. In this chapter, we will delve deeply into the importance of delegating work to the right people. We will start this chapter by looking at the delegation methodology and how it can work for you. We'll then consider two fundamental approaches that you can use to make your team stronger using delegation. Lastly, we'll look at the pros and cons of these methods. Finally, we'll give you a few ideas to communicate effectively as a leader.

We'll close the chapter with some excellent tips for delegation and the way forward. It does sound like it's going to be an exciting journey, doesn't it?

So, let's get started already.

Contents
1. What is delegation?
2. Benefits of delegation
3. Top reasons managers don't delegate
4. How to delegate the right way
5. A step-by-step guide to delegating effectively
6. Control

1. What is delegation?

Delegation usually happens when a manager requests a team member to do a specific task. It's mostly a one-way street, where managers are prone to delegating work. As the manager, you will always be responsible for the task. Delegation is a means to create more time for you to focus on other aspects of management.

For example, if your boss delegates a task to you, your boss is likely still ultimately responsible for making sure that the job is accomplished.

According to Eli Broad, "The inability to delegate is one of the biggest problems...with managers at all levels."

This is an excellent reason as to why managers are ineffective, burned out, and too busy to grow their teams. For example, there was a manager in our sales team who only delegated the difficult tasks that he did not enjoy to this team. So they felt that they were not growing. What usually happens in those teams is that they silently revolt. Soon the productivity decreased, and you're left wondering why. Eli Broad was profound in making that statement, as many leaders do need to start empowering their teams.

2. Benefits of delegation

There are many benefits to delegating, and these will be highlighted below for you.

Gives you more time

Since a lot of your work takes so much time, handing over some of your work to your team could help to alleviate time pressures. With so many things to take care of, time is an essential factor for managers to make strategic decisions for their teams. Many managers spend most of their time at work, don't have much of a social life, and are highly stressed out. Therefore, they could certainly use some time to get more done.

Let's now consider another benefit.

You can focus effectively

It's a known fact that multitasking creates low productivity. If you consider that multitasking is switch tasking, you are often shooting yourself in the foot when you do it. The impact on the quality of your work is vast, and usually, you're so scattered you cannot give the work you're doing your full attention. And as team manager, you may always be in a conversation with staff members discussing clients, coaching, and development. Have you thought, when was the last time you didn't multitask?

Allow your team to develop new skills

There have been many occasions where talented people left organizations due to a lack of growth and development. Staff engagement surveys by the Gallup Organization often feature that managers are the main reason. Lack of growth comes in a close second. The reality is that most managers have so much to do but not enough time in the day to get around to doing it.

That's ok, yet your team ends up disadvantaged due to this. And the exciting thing is that if you realize that your team can make your life easier, you wouldn't be so busy and have a lack of focus. Then your team can help you manage the workload; it builds the engagement in your team and finds sufficient exposure for the talented staff.

You gain a reputation for being an efficient and productive manager
This is an often-overlooked point. Managers also need recognition, and sometimes we focus so intently on staff and ensure they are doing what needs to get done. In essence, we forget that managers need this form of recognition. And as a manager yourself, you can gain this reputation by always being on top of things. Eventually, your colleagues will ask you how you do it, and this could lead to even more recognition from higher management too. All in all, this is a significant factor that could result in you getting a promotion.

Improved communication and trust
Communication is critical when getting your team to buy into a new direction or asking them to do more than they are currently doing. Yet, as you communicate and delegate more to your team, there develops a stronger bond between mentee and mentor, which grows into trust.

It pays to remember that your group enjoys sharing decisive moments, and communication is how we do that. The more you do it, the more trust will build, and your team will even perform better too. This is an advantage of leaping into delegation.

There are so many benefits related to delegation, and often fear holds many managers back. So let's look at fear as the driving force for lack of delegating work.

3. Top reasons managers don't delegate

Fear is, of course, a big one, and that was mentioned in the previous section. And often, it's the driving force behind many of the reasons you will view shortly. This list is not exhaustive but will give you a fair idea of why others are not delegating right now.

Managers have high expectations

Often these managers did delegate in the past, but somehow the work did not turn out the way they wanted, so they had to re-do it. Often these managers do have higher than average expectations and a perfectionist streak too. A good example was a manager who was always a good performer, and he still worked later hours than other managers and was burned out. So much so that he had to take a week off to recover. It seems that his high expectations lead to serious illness. And he needed to decide if his expectations were benefiting him and his team.

They think that their way is the only way

Often this manager has excellent attention to detail, yet is often one-tracked in their thinking and approach. This leads to never delegating as it always ends up being a battle with the person who they delegated to wondering if the person could ever get it right. Generally, these interactions can sour relationships between a manager and his team member. Having an open mind is vital to being a leader.

A general belief that others are incompetent

While they may not admit it, their belief system is one where they think people are not doing their work correctly. It means that they are judging team members on their abilities from the outside without thorough insight. A simple aspect of looking at people more favorably is a step in the right direction to getting this type of manager out of that thinking.

They are not good teachers

We've all seen this show before. A manager is newly appointed from staff level into management, and we then start to see that teaching is not something they are passionate about. And delegating does involve some degree of instruction and showing. The good news is that getting better is something that is in your control. The reality is that practice will always make perfect. You just have to practice a lot more than others. And also, it pays not to compare yourself. That's like comparing yourself to an Olympic medalist when you only just started learning how to swim. Guess what? You will just kill your energy, so steer clear from comparison.

People in their team fear their management style

This is a common one where team members don't benefit much from sessions with their manager. It could be that they have a fearful approach, and their leadership tends to verge on the mean side. Often sarcasm can demoralize a team and not make the team want to contribute or have anything delegated to them. As an example, a team that managed the inbound e-mails of customers had this challenge with their manager. They often gossiped and complained about the situation, but nothing ever changed. Pretty much, the team was trying to get across that the boss did not have many people skills and caused panic and fear during the connect sessions.

You'd imagine it must have been so challenging to have growth conversations when you have a temperamental manager. A good habit to prevent being a sensitive leader is to practice mindfulness.

And yes, many other fears cause a lack of delegation. The only way to recognize this is by asking your manager for feedback on your delegation skills. You may come out learning more than you ultimately thought you would.

Let's now move onto the ways you can delegate more effectively.

4. How to delegate the right way

Delegating the right way is the perfect time to finally learn how to help and support people to feel empowered. Right now, people need extra guidance and support during challenging times.

The first thing you should know is that you always set the tone for your team to follow as the manager, and often expectations are set without you even realizing it.

In an interesting quote by US soldier George S. Patton, he says: "Don't tell people how to do things, tell them what to do, and let them surprise you with their results."

Yet before we attempt delegating, you may have to help people get used to this new thing called delegation. You have to set an expectation and support people into buying into your delegation methods.

Review the experience of a person as well as if they have the capacity and knowledge to get this job done. You may find that the person is quite enthusiastic yet is still mastering her current role. The worst is to challenge an overburdened staff member.

This only results in failure in the delegation process and mental trauma over delegation for the staff member. On the other end of the spectrum, you may have a top performer who is bored and needs to be challenged.

Then choose this person for incredible results. But also give this person a test to check if they could do it well. It could be something along the lines of the work yet at a lower level. See how the person reacts to the challenge, and if the person does a good job or not. But please don't provide hurtful feedback if you don't get the desired result. Remember, you were a beginner once before too.

Consider the way this person works in the office. In many more prominent companies, there are so many roles available for entry-level jobs, and most people take it because they don't yet possess the skills to apply for other positions. But the good news is that this person may have a great attitude, so they are ultimately teachable.

And a person with a proper mindset but low skills will always be better than someone who has an inferior mindset and excellent work. And usually, in these cases, they do not want to work extra.

They pretty much come in, do their job, and leave. An excellent way to get to know your team is to look for essential aspects like the person's long term goals, why do they like working for the team, and also what are things they do in their spare time. It could give you an idea of their suitability for the job.

You never want to give someone more work when they already have so much to do. A good rule of thumb is to help support them with getting their work done first before delegating. You will find that this person simply does not have time to take on more work.

On the other hand, perhaps delegating to them would bring the best results, so why not shuffle some of the work around so that you can delegate to them. The bonus is that you will have more confidence in the person's ability to do the job. And it will help them do better too.

Many experienced managers know all too well how the first delegation could lead to some rather alarming findings, and good managers understand that the work will not be done correctly. And the best way to move past that is to ensure that you are patient and helpful as they learn a new skill.

Let's look at a step by step process to delegating effectively without pulling all your hair out.

5. A step-by-step guide to delegate effectively

Step 1: Make sure that you know what you want. This process could be in the form of an example, or you may have a well-drafted plan of how to do a task. Always know what the end goal will look like. If you have to, print out a copy or share it as an e-mail with clear instructions.

Step 2: Think about what the person may need during this process. For example, if they have to create a report for you, make sure they have access to all of the programs such as Excel or other analytical types of applications.

Step 3: Set down some ground rules. This simply means expectations of what is needed, as well as the rules of engagement. Many times you find that people don't know when to approach the manager for advice and sit in silence as the deadline looms. This is not exactly helpful and sure to be a recipe for disaster.

At this stage, you want to consider making it clear that you're available for questions and concerns and that there is no such thing as a 'silly' question. Explain to the person that things will not always be perfect, but if they share their challenges, you could provide some useful advice.

Step 4: Always remind yourself that yes, you can delegate tasks and some authority, but at the end of the day, you are responsible for the outcome of the delegated work. And if it is possible, aim to delegate to someone who understands the nitty-gritty of the work, preferably someone who has done the task or has vast standing knowledge about it. This will be sure to make the person more confident, and they will deliver exceptional results too.

Step 5: Be supportive and remember to provide clarity and be ever ready to answer questions. A big no-no is dumping the work on the person and expecting them to figure it out. There is a level of 'question asking' needed to make sense of a task for a beginner, so aim to help them out by supporting them with all the necessary resources and tools.

Step 6: Do not micromanage the person. It can be quite demoralizing. Give them the work and ask for results instead and give them milestones to hit.

When they bring the results, consider it together, and ensure that you are both satisfied. If you do have feedback, then make sure you package it in the right way so that they use that feedback to improve. Doing this will build trust, and the relationship and communication will grow along the way.

Step 7: Remember that motivation is fundamental to someone who is starting to learn a new skill. A good idea would be to review the work at every milestone and find positives that will help show your appreciation for the person. And help them grow as well, and give them reasons why this work is so important, help them find meaning and purpose in the work they are doing. Remember, great leaders always start with the why, and this builds commitment from the team along the way.

If you've followed the above steps, you would be moving in the right direction. You have an empowered member of your team that is learning new skills, you have more work being done, and you also have more time to focus on the more strategic aspects of your role as a manager instead of putting out fires all day.

Let's wrap up this chapter by looking at a massively important factor - namely: How do you maintain the work standards and ensure it is consistent when you delegate to a team member?

And the answer to that is, of course: control.

6. Control

The word control, in this sense, is used as a means to check that everything is on track with the person you delegated to. Of course, you shouldn't micromanage, but you should have some idea of how the personal is tracking with the work.

Here are a few tips to help you do that:
- Set up a recurring meeting to check in on the project, look at what's been done so far, and provide feedback around your expectations.
- Make sure that you discuss when the project is due, and set expectations of a good time of receiving it and the condition of the work.
- Even though you did delegate this work, don't leave it without review. Review it and discuss areas that were good and areas of improvement too.

In this chapter, our goal was delegating to the right people for success. And we found that we have to look at a few options when it comes to people that may be suited for the work. You can do this by observing the team. Then, discuss during your connect sessions with each member of the group.

There is an art to delegation, but with some patience, you can get better every single day. Soon, you will be delegating like a pro. Let's take a giant leap towards communication.

4 ESTABLISH A COMMUNICATION MODEL

So far, we have considered planning as a team manager and delegation to master effective team management.

Yet, the next step on our journey links to communication and how you can use it to be a more effective manager

Contents
1. Why is effective communication critical?
2. Communicate directly with team members
3. Benefits of using direct messaging
4. How do great managers communicate?
5. Tools to help you communicate better

1. Why is effective communication critical?
There is clarity and understanding

When managers communicate effectively, they have set a bright tone of what's expected, and there is never misunderstanding and confusion in the team. This is great as it fosters positive working relationships and also helps to build a pleasant working environment.

Some time ago, a manager who was relatively new to the situation was getting many complaints about their style of communication. The team felt the manager was not sharing as much detail as they would like.

Consequently, they could not do the work to the best of their ability, and the manager was hindering the team. In this example, you can see that the manager used their preferred style of communication.

At the same time, the team wanted a different, more detailed form of communication. The communication styles did not match, and conflict ensued.

And that's where communication genuinely becomes so essential. Remember, when your team is hearing your messaging but cannot fully grasp the contents, you may have lost half the battle of team management. An excellent remedy for this is to practice sharing messages with detail-oriented colleagues or ask the most detailed-oriented team member to probe you with questions for more detail.

As long as you don't get defensive and answer professionally, it should give valuable insights to your team. Let's consider another reason excellent communication is crucial.

You avoid misunderstanding

When there is excellent communication, you don't leave things open to interpretation. You should always actively share a message instead of leaving it to fester. Better to communicate directly and be as transparent as possible for the best results.

Teamwork is more prevalent

When a manager communicates the vision of the company, the team is likely to resonate and rally around doing great things to build the team and become more successful together. This often helps the organization become more creative, thoughtful, and open to change. All in all, it affects the team and the overall sustainability of the company.

More satisfied customers

Happy customers become the new norm. If all the managers are aligned with the business's message and communicate effectively, then policies and procedures are carried out effectively, and customers always get the same standard of service.

2. Communicate directly with team members

When many personalities get together, this has the potential to cause disagreements due to a clash of personalities. It's so important to understand that direct communication in the team is vital. When the unit is not communicating straightforwardly with each other, it usually signals something more profound is wrong.

As the team manager, you should always be aware of indirect communication and find tools to curb this as soon as possible.

What happens when team members use indirect communication?

There was a case of this where there was a disagreement between two team members, and during a meeting, they had a mini argument. After this, it severely affected their working relationship so much so that they were not communicating directly anymore. Over time messages were being passed via another person to reach this person.

This is a classic case of conflict management gone wrong. And if left to simmer, it could lead to factions in the team, where people have to choose sides. Eventually, it leads to a team that has poor working relationships, and it becomes an unpleasant place to work in.

Another reason this impacts the team is that people are avoiding conflict. They should always remember that we will never agree on everything, and if we do then, there may be something wrong. Disagreements are an opportunity to invoke new and fresh ways to think and do exciting projects. It's how teams move forward and become successful.

In fact, in the excellent book 'crucial conversations' they say: "The single biggest problem in communication is the illusion that it has taken place."

And isn't it so real? Often when people in your team choose not to speak to each other about a problem, it only gets bigger. And in a work context, it has the opportunity to explode into something bigger than it needs to be. As the leader in the team, you should teach your team members how to handle conflict well.

A good idea is to use real-life examples during your discussion or check-in sessions with your team members. Perhaps you had a few instances where you avoided conflict, and things did not turn out the way you planned for it to turn out. This practical example could even serve as a teaching tool during your next team meeting. And your team members will thank you because they have learned valuable skills in managing conflict and keeping the communication channel open.

Consider using technology to improve communication in the team
Gone are the days when e-mail was the only source of communication. We have so many options available that we are spoiled for choice. Yet, as a manager, you shouldn't shy away from using faster ways of communicating, such as WhatsApp, Slack, Skype, or any instant chat service that keeps communication channels fast-paced.

By incorporating technology into the work environment, projects start to move fast, so you no longer have to wait hours for the go-ahead. You can now simply text the person and get a yes, no, or maybe. This is great for getting things done, making the overall team more productive and overall great for you as the manager who can always get fast communication from your team.

Often you may find that you need a quick answer on a question to move an essential project to its result. If you use e-mail, you'd have to wait hours to get a response since people tend to check their e-mails less often. And if you decide to use Skype or Slack, the answer would come a lot faster.

3. Benefits of using direct messaging
Direct messages can be used when you send messages via Skype or Slack. This is a fast and effective way to communicate and get what you want.

Encourages brainstorming

Since it's so quick, you can have ideas flowing faster, resulting in more inspiration for the project at hand. It could also lead to solving other problems that you did not think of before. And this could lead to new and exciting plans for the team.

Updates are frequent

Instead of having to wait till someone sees your last e-mail, which might be right at the bottom of the pile since you sent it in the morning - you can choose to send a direct message instead. And the chances of that person ignoring you is pretty slim. And that's how you get your work done more effectively as a manager too.

Video calls can be beneficial

Another great tool since you can simply video call and have a face to face experience instead. This is preferred for more intricate discussions which don't seem to be gaining any traction over e-mail or messaging. Seeing a person on the other side can also prompt more empathy for situations in the team. It's a great way to communicate with virtual teams.

Less e-mail

And you know how much e-mail can be flooded. Do you recall seeing colleagues with over 50000 e-mails unread in their inbox? That's truly scary, but it's not going to get better unless we make an effort to stop sending unnecessary e-mails. Working with a manager that continually sends unnecessary e-mails can be tiring, so ensure that you find alternative means to communicate.

Things to consider when using direct messaging for work communication

While there are many benefits for a team to use direct messaging, it can sometimes have a few disadvantages:

- **Expectations:** Once you start receiving instantaneous responses, it becomes an expectation, and it puts everyone on high alert, trying to respond as quickly as possible. People may get upset if you don't respond as quickly, especially considering you're receiving a pop-up message every time the message comes through. Therefore, you do need to let people know that you may not always answer as quickly as you might be busy with an important task.

- **Easy to lose focus:** Let's face it, we love to chat to our colleagues and have fun instead of working. Yet, we have to stay focused if we are to finish our work for the day. When you have a messenger app on your computer, then pop up's can certainly be worrisome. And they take you away from what you were trying to complete, and it takes so long to get back on track. To curb this, aim to put your notifications for the messenger service off. This will help you gain back your focus.

- **You get unnecessary questions:** Often, you will find that people send you questions they could have answered themselves by researching the topics. This is also very distracting for the team and can stall all sorts of progress that was made previously. An excellent way to approach the situation would be to engage the team directly and have an open discussion about question asking and the impact on the team.

Overall the pros always outweigh the cons of direct messaging team members for help, but it's vital to keep monitoring the situation and address any anomalies related to direct messaging.

Now that we've looked at forms of communication and different types of communication a manager may deal with. Let's consider how to communicate effectively as a manager to get the results you so desire.

4. How do great managers communicate?
They meet their employees regularly

This is one of the most critical factors. This relationship-building is crucial for the working relationship to thrive. If your team knows about your expectations and you know about theirs, then the engagement at work is much better. There is less misunderstanding, and you're always on top of everything surrounding that team's performance, growth, and career development. This is one of the proven ways to improve how engaged people are at their jobs.

Another significant factor is that you always have sight of how to help them if their work standards have dropped, and you can avoid moving into a disciplinary discussion involving the HR team.

They always let their teams know what's going on

This idea of keeping the team in the loop is vital and a great way to build the team's trust and respect over time. In doing so, you will get their buy-in for changes coming their way; you can prepare them for business changes and give them resources to manage their work better. And the best part is that they will use the information, knowing that it is coming from a valuable source who has been transparent with the team. On the other end of the spectrum, a poor manager always keeps the team in the dark and leaves them feeling tired, confused, and out of the loop.

A great idea is to have a weekly team meeting, and share all of the updates at the moment that you feel your team needs to know.

They don't fear feedback
Managers can worry about feedback from their team, thinking it will show them in a bad light. It's never the case as feedback is a valuable tool that we can use to learn and grow. The more we get feedback, the easier it is to understand what's right and what's important to consider but unhelpful. Generally, you will always have one or two people in the team that no matter what you do, they will never have anything positive to say.

That's not what you should be focusing on. Focus on the rest of the team who are positive, engaged, and happy and then support the team members that aren't. Make them see the impact they have on the team. Remember that it's vital to share feedback with your team. This feedback could range from work performance to behavior to compliments. It's really up to you, but you must do it.

5. Tools to help you communicate better

We're not all born skilled communicators. But the good news is that you can learn to improve. In doing so, you will get better over time.

A great place to improve your communication skills is to join Toastmasters. They are a great place that helps leaders improve how they get their message across. They have weekly sessions where they engage, give speeches, and practice saying an address in front of a crowd.

Also, aim to get a mentor that can show you where your communication skills are not hitting the mark. This external view can help you start building your communication skills.

Practice truly does make perfect, so always be prepared when you have to communicate with your team by taking down the notes during your meetings and cross-checking the information.

And like we touched on in this chapter, use alternative means of communication like Slack, WhatsApp, or Skype to share your message and keep in touch.

Communicating a message isn't always easy; you would agree, but we have to start establishing valid communication models for our teams to thrive and for you to improve your team's performance over time.

We've mentioned a few ideas and suggestions to communicate effectively as well as practical ways to do better every day.

Now it's your turn to go out and practice these skills.

5 ESTABLISH A COLLABORATION MODEL

In this chapter, we'll discuss establishing a collaboration model. Your role as a team manager should be to ensure people work together to meet the goals of the organization or business. To do this, team members must collaborate. This collaboration, led by the team manager, is also vital for building high performing teams.

Many of the areas we touched on in the previous sections should iron out many issues related to collaboration. In this final chapter, we'll bed down the successful tools that will be incredibly useful to you to ensure that your teams work together, build good team spirit and have massive success at work and personally, too.

Contents

1. Benefits of team collaboration

2. Barriers to collaboration and solutions
3. Establishing a model for collaboration

Let's begin by reviewing the benefits of team collaboration.

1. Benefits of team collaboration

Flexibility in the company

Flexibility directly relates to being agile enough to adjust to changes that happen around you. And you should have the ability to go ahead and do this calmly and professionally.

You will find that you may need to rework all outputs. Flexibility is all about changing direction when you least expect it and doing great work despite this. In organizations, there are so many changes that occur every minute, and teams must deal with it appropriately.

And as a manager, you must ensure that your team does this effectively without breaking anything along the way. Many organizations are heavily dependent on collaboration and people working together to get the job done.

Here are two examples where collaboration will be necessary:
- You have a new team member that needs up-skilling on the processes in your team, and you have limited availability at present. You then have to seek help from the group to assist with the work.
- Alternatively, one of your team members has just called in sick, and their load of work needs urgent attention. Your next step is to call upon the team for help.

These two examples indicate how collaboration can support the team amidst challenging situations.

There's a saying in companies that the only constant is change. Therefore, it infers that people within the organization must adapt and do so quickly. Yet, the only way to adapt to change is to embrace collaboration. When solo work occurs, it makes it that much more challenging to pivot best practice across the board during disruptive technologies or sudden emergencies in your industry. If there is a culture of collaboration, things move more seamlessly with less friction. In work methodologies like agile, the fundamental principle is flexibility and responsiveness. And usually, with greater flexibility, you will find that another benefit becomes apparent.

Good employee sentiment
A recent Gallup study found that 78% of engaged workers believe their work lives benefit them psychologically. Perhaps you also find this is interesting, yet it gives you a clear understanding of how vital collaboration is in the workplace. Often when collaboration is weak, it affects employee morale and productivity. This aspect could result in poor communication, office politics, gossip, or unfair work distribution.

Let's consider John, a quality assessor, who was a star performer. He consistently hit the goals required and was someone that always went above and beyond in his role. Yet, the divisional manager in the area noticed he had declined in performance, so the manager spoke to the team manager to find out what could be the problem.

The team manager shared some vital information. He explained that there had been some collaboration issues in the team due to a new team member who was not pulling their weight.

Due to this and the lack of accountability for other team members, John started to do the bare minimum. The team manager engaged with the team and discussed the issues with each team member. There had since been a marked improvement, and collaboration had improved significantly. This example of employee sentiment being affected by cooperation or the lack thereof is quite common. Yet, the opposite is true as well. When employees are collaborating and working towards the goals of the organization, it becomes much easier to operate as a team.

Therefore, managers must foster collaboration and remove barriers to collaboration. Building teamwork also improves team spirit and camaraderie. And this, of course, leads to fully engaged team members eager to do more, take on new projects, and who embrace changes. Engaged employees make meetings that much more productive, as you will see in the next point.

Productive meetings
When you have efficient collaboration with your team, you will be pleased to see that your team meetings run well, and you get more done.
This aspect is because there is ongoing teamwork that is fueling employees to engage at every turn proactively. You then need fewer meetings to resolve disagreements, conflicts, and to make simple decisions.

Further, you have a culture that supports meetings and with less hidden agendas too. Each team member is more engaged, supportive of one another, and wants to do more in the actual meeting.

Unproductive meetings waste more than $37 billion per year, according to Muse, and executives view 73% of meetings as a failure. Overall collaboration could be the key to enhanced meetings and significant cost savings too.

Higher retention rates

While collaboration doesn't directly impact this metric, it can lead to higher retention rates in your team. You will have engaged and happy employees who are fulfilled by the work they do. Due to this, employees do not spend time searching for new employment.

They find that collaboration allows them to do their best work, improve working relationships, and creates a harmonious environment.

You will be surprised to find that people would prefer staying at an organization that makes them happy as opposed to going elsewhere that increases their revenue. Meanwhile, employee disengagement can lead to you losing your top talent who will leave for better work prospects. Speaking of which, let's consider another benefit that is often overlooked.

More innovation

Since more of the team is collaborating, sharing, and working together, a symbiotic idea sharing takes place.

More innovation allows for various thoughts and ideas to take form and flight. Due to this, employees start considering ways to improve your standard operating procedures to reduce costs. This process also leads to better methods, happier clients, and an overly exciting place to work in that is always on the cutting edge.

According to the Gallup survey, a positive relationship exists between work performance and engagement at work. People who feel more connected to their work show increased productivity.

This also leads to more loyalty for the company and enthusiasm for their work. And naturally improves collaboration with coworkers, and this starts to play out in the innovation field leading to higher profitability.

Increase the profitability of your company
It's intuitive that if employees are engaged, happy, and collaborating; then it will affect the bottom line of your company in a very positive way.

The original mix of collaboration with the best people who are engaged means more innovative solutions. People working without any barriers are significantly better at getting the job done as quickly as possible.

Let's consider the next aspect of collaboration that could ultimately prevent you from reaching your team's goals. By this, we mean the barriers to collaboration.

2. Barriers to collaboration and solutions
Lack of respect and trust
At times, there will be less respect and trust evident within a team, and you will notice the difference. You will find team members hoard information, complain for no real reason, and also there is more tension than needed in the workplace.

Thinking back to a situation where Janine in one of our teams was a new hire. She entered the team to support project management. Yet, her initial interactions with team members were not optimal, and many felt she lacked the necessary respect when engaging with them. There were many complaints, and the team refused to work with her.

Lack of collaboration resulted in delayed communication channels and barriers to moving forward on projects.

Mostly meetings were held to fix the relational challenges, and the work stood by the wayside. These are symptoms of a perception of a lack of respect and trust in a team.

Often there might be team members similar to Janine in your teams who do not have the insight that they are doing anything wrong. Although other team members will disagree, and these relationship fallouts will impact your team negatively. This scenario is due to different belief systems and ideas about respect, and the perception thereof.

Solution: In this example, the manager engaged with Janine directly, and found that she thought she was perfectly well-toned with everyone and shared that the rest of the team was often late and showed no respect towards her. Therefore, it became a 'he said she said' scenario. As a solution, a team meeting took place to get everyone on the same page as to Janine's role and each team member's role.

From here, a weekly connect session as a team took place to discuss, share, and also break the ice so that the team could get to know each other.

This example is a clear one where increased levels of interaction are required, and it should be as direct as possible so that new employees can understand the culture of the environment and allow a time frame for making changes. Understanding team roles are vital and recommended.

These are a few ideas to help you out:

- Ensure regular engagement between team members who perform different functions, and ensure they know what each role's responsibilities include.
- Connect sessions weekly with all employees to understand their challenges and areas which need development.
- Keep an eye on team meetings, and look for areas where there may be hidden agendas afoot. Disruptive meetings would be a symptom. Engage with the affected parties and move forward.
- Always set the tone and bring the vision to your team's attention. It's a good idea to display the vision in documents, meetings, and strategy sessions.

These ideas will be sure to bring a newfound understanding of roles in the team, as well as create open communication while developing respectful and trusting relationships between peers. Likely this will be a starting point to build a model for collaboration.

Differences in mindset

When working with people, it pays to remember that there will always be different mindsets, ideas, and beliefs. And of course, trying to change people's opinions is quite challenging, and there are many approaches available to help you.

An excellent way to think about mindsets is that it can be molded and shaped, provided the team member is willing to play a role in cooperating. Frequently when an employee mindset is beyond repair, it also may mean that keeping them around reduces the productivity of your team and company. The reality is that a poor mindset may truly cripple the vision of the team and where it's headed, leading to unnecessary complications along the way.

Generally speaking, when the organization's vision and the team members' values are so misaligned that you have to do something urgently, then it's better to go ahead and do it sooner rather than later.

Yet if it has to get to that stage, you can still salvage the situation with a few pointed actions.

Solution: Always remember that you can still act despite how bad the situation has become when differing mindsets are involved—the word being 'act'.

You will find below a host of ideas to get everyone onto the same page so you can move forward as a team:

- Create a safe working space where team members don't feel judged in any sense, and this will ensure they are contributing their best ideas and work.
- Keep an open mind as the manager. Aim to look at all sides of a problem even if it goes against your convictions personally. You must always engage professionally and objectively.
- Aim not to take sides, and fairly mediate any conflict that ensues.
- And importantly, ensure that criticism or feedback gets relayed with the utmost care and attention.
- Always remember that everyone is different in the way they think. Your method of viewing the world is simply that. Everyone has new, exciting, and varied viewpoints that could help create diverse thinking.

- That said, knowing this aspect means you can see how well the team can do when various strengths, perspectives, and ideas get shared. As the manager, you should harness this power.
- Aim to have more brainstorming sessions which deliberately trigger differing opinions, and let the team know you're doing this to open up the floor for various discussions in a respectful manner. Monitor the situation, step in where needed, and share a feedback loop after around what worked, what needed improvement, and the focus area for the next brainstorm session.
- Be open to new ideas and show team members that you value all opinions by validating, using, or sharing these with upper management where possible.

Poor listening skills

Some people listen with the intent to respond or defend a viewpoint. In this case, their listening skills are not at the level it needs to be. Managers and their teams must make it a top priority to listen appropriately. In the absence of active listening, you will miss out on valuable information that people are sharing that will help move the team towards its goals. Yet, it's true it gets busy, and sometimes multitasking starts to rear its ugly head, or generally, you're not that good at listening, and much prefer doing.

A case in point is a manager who was the head of debt management and had a knack for always responding inappropriately to questions. He often seemed like he would intently listen. Yet, his answer to employee questions did not hit the mark as it should, resulting in disgruntled employees. These employees were also disengaged in meetings and even confused about the work that needed to get done. To add to the matter, all strategy efforts from higher management got lost in translation. The team had to seek out information through the grapevine. Eventually, the manager in question had a team that would not do what needed to be done or collaborate effectively.

Can you guess what could have happened here?

It would seem that the manager had poor listening skills, always aiming to say something without taking the time to comprehend these questions. Employees still want to feel heard and understood and may forgive you the first few times, but their patience wears thin over time. Ultimately the situation leads to a lack of understanding, clarity, and, consequently, limited collaboration.

Solution: Having a manager that does not listen well can be challenging, yet you could say the same for employee's that have poor listening skills. Yet, this is hardly ever an intentional challenge; at times, people take in information differently to others. Due to this, they hear what they need to, digest it, then supply the feedback. The only way for managers and employees to truly fix this situation is to ensure that you always check for clarity. You check for clarity by asking questions such as "Please may I clarify your point." or "I would like to be clear about what you're asking." These questions and statements are steps in the right direction, and team members will welcome them as it shows you are trying to help.

And for employees that have trouble with listening skills in meetings or when engaging, you must understand the root of the problem. Finding the source of the problem is simple to do. It takes effort in observing the staff member in action. You have to confirm that they are not distracted by their phone, other personal matters, or if it's a once-off thing. This step will be helpful overall.

Here are a few more tangible ideas:
- Always be fully present when engaging with the team; make this your top priority.
- Be open-minded, and remember that opinions differ, and listening is a tool to find solutions to problems you may not know existed.
- Take notes if necessary, and be active in your listening, trying to find the meaning behind the word instead of jumping to conclusions.
- Look at tone, body language, and facial expressions and mirror these to suit the conversation at hand.
- Show empathy towards the speaker.
- Do not multitask as team members see this as disrespectful.
- Focus on what the speaker is saying instead of intending to respond.
- Aim to summarise the conversation at the end to make sure you received everything the speaker was trying to get across.
- Use clarifying questions with care and don't interrupt speakers.

Gaps in knowledge

Generally, this occurs when teams have no basic understanding of the work their peers do. This situation may be due to being too busy on your own work, or too lazy to find out. Since the team members lack a typical frame of reference, they will find it challenging to work together for the common goal of the team.

And generally, information can be hard to find about the topics. Also, it takes time and effort to understand a function. At times, individuals with specific skill sets may look down upon another skillset and think the knowledge is not worth learning.

Consequently, in meetings, you will find time wasters as people clarify and fail to grasp the context of the sessions, and therefore solutions are slow to form.

Solution: The ultimate answer is to up-skill the team on everything, yet this is not always viable due to time constraints and other requirements. So the best way is to broaden your frame of reference and consider other avenues.

Here's how to fix this challenge:
- Make it a duty to understand other areas or functions in your team, especially those that directly affect your work. You may find a case for interaction between managers and developers is essential when discussing the customer journey.
- Offer training for team members who require core information from a skillset.
- Make pairs of people from other disciplines so they can work together. Do this through a shared project and incentivize them with prizes.
- Create a central repository, and share the knowledge of the team, use this information once a month and highlight something important in your team meetings. Make sure you reward people for sharing.
- Empower team members to own the knowledge repository and especially those who are looking to grow in the company.
- Share a monthly newsletter from various skill sets and business areas.

Internal competition

Competition is vital in a team as it motivates people to do their best work. Yet, at times, it can derail important work your team is doing as people's own agenda's surface. You will notice signs of this when people keep valuable information a secret so they can be looked upon favorably for the next promotion.

Also, this competition can result in cliques within the team, creating factions and derailing all the efforts to create a performing and collaborative team.

Solution: This is always challenging as competition can make things better in many ways, so explain to the team that healthy competition is good. Yet, at this stage, the focus is on ensuring the team helps and supports each other.

Here are a few tangible tips:
- Create a team vision and have everyone contribute and ensure that the value around collaboration is front and center.
- Host a strategy session and list the topic of competition and how it can be detrimental to the team.
- Leverage individuals who are the most competitive and give them a project to discuss the benefits and drawbacks of competition in the group. Have these persons also engage with other team members around the impact of competitive behavior.
- During the meeting, always emphasize the need to share information and collaborate.
- Model collaborative behaviors with other team managers.

Now that you have a clear idea around the benefits and barriers of collaboration, it will be vital that we explore more solutions to enhancing cooperation through a collaboration model.

3. Establishing a model for collaboration

As a first step, you must decide to create a plan for collaboration in your team both when you're there and when you are not.

Throughout this chapter, we've looked in-depth at the barriers and benefits of collaboration, and we saw how vital it was to your success and the success of your business. Yet we failed to look at the critical steps needed to foster collaboration from start to finish.

It pays to remember that teams work toward a similar goal that will benefit all parties involved. Generally, teamwork goes hand in hand with collaboration. It merely means that many different people came together to achieve a goal and serve a purpose.

And we know intuitively that the strength of a team comes from supporting one another and ensuring you communicate to the best of your ability.

You may also consider that some groups share the same skills, while other teams may have a variety of skill sets housed together for a business purpose or goal.

Usually, if a team is lacking in an area, then as the manager, you can apply a team-building effort to get everyone onto the same page, bring them closer together, and have them do the work as best as possible.

MASTER EFFECTIVE TEAM MANAGEMENT

This explanation gives you a background of how most teams operate and will help your teams get to a stage of teamwork and collaboration, which is essentially where the magic happens.

Collaboration, therefore, can be broken down into four factors:

Communication: Communication is another critical element of working together as a team. All team members must make it a priority to engage and talk to each other. This could mean many more fruitful engagement sessions, and as the team manager, you should take the lead.

Cooperation: Cooperation is an integral element of collaboration. It requires that every team member is on board and moving full steam ahead with the agreed business needs. It requires that everyone believes in the end goal and plays their part.

Coordination: This activity is all about the details and ensuring each process is completed and on time. It needs every team member to play their role and do the work effectively. It also requires the team manager to make spot checks to ensure satisfactory completion.

This activity leads to ultimate efficiency by ensuring team members have a roadmap for what they need to do:

Teamwork: Teamwork generally happens when all the stages of communication, coordination, and cooperation are passed and leads to the team working and moving together. Ultimately, this results in a positive result leading to increased levels of productivity, collaboration, and profitability for your business.

This model is an excellent way to get everyone on board and stick to the vision ahead. It requires lots of cohesion with everyone on board and going in the same direction.

It's time to go through each of the steps in this model.

You should consider these ideas on how to get your team on board and raring to go:

Communication

Granted you followed along in the previous section, you would know that we covered communication intensely as a tool that will help to get all members on board.

In this section, we'll look at communication from a different perspective. We know that communication refers to how people send out and receive messages. And naturally, an excellent communicator will be able to use and sense verbal and nonverbal cues, be an active listener while also employing empathy. Communication is, in fact, a soft skill. And the reason for this name is that you use it to build rapport and goodwill in your organization. A great communicator will always get their point across in a simple and easy to understand way. It helps teams understand what they need to do, so they can get it done hassle-free.

Therefore good communicators will:
- Ensure that the topic at hand is related to the person with whom they are engaging.
- Create a space where authenticity can thrive and provide factual information.
- Provide all the necessary details in the shortest time as possible.

- Check for clarity to gain understanding.
- Ensure that it is a top priority to listen attentively to the content of the messages shared.
- Look for areas of discomfort which could impact the conversation down the line.

There are also typical scenarios where communication of the plan of action will be vital to ensure maximum collaboration in your team. As an example, consider that there is an emergency shut down of work systems on the last day of the month, and that is your busiest period.

Therefore, as the team manager, you need all hands on deck before the shutdown. Communicating this message becomes vital to a successful end of the month and the start of the new month.

How do you go about communicating this message?

Know your facts: When the message gets passed down from upper management, then ensure that you are listening attentively. You should find the five factors such as Who, What, How, Why, and When of the message. You may even consider writing each answer to the question to make sure you don't miss anything.

Ask all the right questions: Though it may seem daunting to ask so many questions during an emergency, you must do so if needed. Remember, these are the questions your team will eventually pose to you. You will receive massive push-back if you don't have satisfactory answers.

Remain calm: Most managers don't remain composed enough to share a coherent message, and this is a sure-fire way to lose your team's confidence.

Yes, it may be busy, and there is an emergency, but panic does not help the situation. A rule of thumb is always to remain calm, remember the facts, and be confident in the information that you're sharing.

Always start with the reason: When you do set up a meeting with your team, it's good to share the reason for the emergency, share how it will impact the business unit as well as the impact over the short term or long term. The initial stage is that you want to share info directly related to the business unit, and give as much information as possible.

Field questions: Once you share the information, prepare for any questions, and patiently provide the answers. Avoid getting overly defensive with your more assertive employees. And give as much detail as possible.

And finally, if you don't have an answer, admit that you will get back to the team. Once you find the solution, get back to the group via e-mail, or face to face.

Check for understanding: Every team member will take in information differently, and some are better listeners than others. Always clarify your message and summarise what you've said. This process will ensure that those who did not fully grasp the situation will start to make those connections.

Document and delegate: Once you complete the message and the team is on the same page; it's time to list the key actions stemming from your meeting. Meeting minutes are a great way to hold your team accountable and a reinforcement of the message that was shared.

Offer your support: A great way to end a meeting of any communication scenario is to end on a good note. This note could be to share the great work the team has been doing, and how far each team member has come so far. Show the team what good work looks like and give thanks for their understanding and commitment. Share transparently the actions you will be taking to support the team and also ask, "What can I do to help?".
The team is responsible for their work, that's true. Yet, help could be that you do not increase their workload. You could also extend the deadlines for projects due.

This process should be the right path for communicating a message that urgently needs to be shared and for your team to start taking action. Notice how at every stage, you build up and get the team on board through sharing openly and also showing your team a willingness to help. Notice that you are there to support the team to move forward. The tone and the messaging is one of support, care, and also holding the team accountable positively and engagingly. This leads us to focus on the cooperation stage.

Cooperation
Let's move into the next stage as we model collaboration effectively. The good news is that if you communicated expertly, then you will get more buy-in from your team. This show's in work put out, as well as the attitude and general team sentiment.

A team that is not willing to cooperate is one where minimal work gets done, and the work delivered is of mediocre quality. Many factors contribute to a lack of cooperation, and generally, it relates to the team engagement, motivation, and sentiment at the time.

As the familiar adage goes, a happy team will always do more than expected while an unhappy team will do everything possible to do as little as possible. You should plan effectively for your team to cooperate with you. As an example, your team should have regular engagement with you as the manager which builds up good rapport over time. This will feed into a positive working relationship.

In this section, you will get the opportunity to understand the factors that influence cooperation in your team and practical ways to always have a highly co-operative team. Let's look at the first factor.

Team engagement: Never underestimate the importance of a highly engaged team. A highly engaged will always do more than expected, and do so with a smile. The engagement can stem from many factors, including job proficiency, positive working relationships, excellent remuneration, and harmonious work-life balance. An engaged team includes engaged, optimistic team members. And as the manager, you must make sure you engage with your team as frequently as possible. Let's take an example of a new team. A new group that recently formed has not built any relationships; therefore, as the manager, your first point of call should be to start building working relationships with every member of the team.

Coaching sessions: While you may be the manager of the team and running the day to day operations, you do need to wear the hat of the leader to ensure there is cooperation from your team members. It starts with coaching sessions. During these sessions, you can discuss where the person is at the current stage in their career.

You can also consider where they hope to be in the future. This option is an excellent opportunity to get to know your team members and also find areas of improvement for them, and you can offer support and advice in a non-abrasive way. If you set the tone right in this session, you will find that your team member is open to trusting you and would see the merit in following through on team requirements.

Team buildings: Yes, many teams think this is a fun day that they get to be with their friends and chat. That's quite true, yet it's also an opportunity that you get to bring your team together in a different setting. Significant team buildings can teach effective collaboration and help you learn more about each team member's strengths and areas of improvement. This opportunity is vital for each team member to connect and build rapport. And this can be carried over to the work you do. An excellent way to host a team-building is to create activities designed to bring the team closer together and build a competitive element into the mix as well.

Recruitment: At times, you may find that you would need to recruit for your team. And this daunting task can make or break a group. Hiring the right person to fit the culture of a high performing team is vital. A sole individual can indeed single-handedly break the synergy of a team. It's a great idea to look widely for candidates, and then shortlist only the best people that you know will fit into the vision of your team and gel well with the current team members. Most importantly, understand the strengths needed in your organization, and bring in a person to fill those gaps.

Onboarding: Once you've recruited the right team members, it's time to make sure that the team members understand the values of the team as well as the expectations. In doing so, this will ensure that all new team members know the requirements from the get-go. And it sets the tone for them and provides the necessary support for their new work journey. Most new team members take time to learn the ropes, and you have to help them along with an onboarding process.

In the last stages of the model, you must consider the best coordination factors that will ensure that the team runs smoothly. Generally, when you reach this stage as a team, you are gunning for the spot of teamwork and collaboration. And you would be moving towards the stage of being called a high performing team.

Yet, what goes into excellent coordination, and how can you support this process?

Coordination
Coordination is making sure that the right things happen at the right time to achieve your overall outcome. This point is where the details are vital to success.

And while we're moving closer to the buzzword known as teamwork, and your dreams of assembling an unstoppable team drives you forward, remember to consider a few aspects before rushing ahead. In reality, getting to such a stage is quite challenging.

There are so many moving parts, and it takes hard work to keep everyone coordinated. That said, it's not impossible provided you have the right tools.

Keep the following in mind when coordinating a team:

Big picture thinking: As the captain of the ship, always keep the big goal or your vision, as we discussed in chapter 1 in mind. Planning is truly all about getting those details together, and you always need to know that it fits into the vision for your team. Think of your team putting pieces of a puzzle together. The goal is to get a beautiful picture at the end. This picture is your vision. At times you have to go down into the details. But come back to look at the big picture. Doing this will help you create concise and clear action plans for the way forward.

Well-defined roles: People on your team need to know their exact responsibilities. If they don't, they will be confused and worn out from trying to do everything. Ensure that before you bring new people into your team, you set out the scope for their role and the specific tasks that are required. And always be updating as you engage with the person. It is vital to know the areas of improvement and strengths of your team. A great tool that many companies use is called Strengthsfinder. The Gallup Organisation created this tool to help you find the strengths for members of your team or company. This tool will give you a sense as to who will be suitable for various tasks that keep your company running.

Plan to succeed: The worst idea is to figure things out as you go, you're only inviting trouble. To be successful, you must know what your objectives are and track these metrics weekly, monthly, and bi-annually.

Know the tasks required from each team member and the resources associated. There can be flexibility and an openness to change, but it's a good idea to keep some semblance of structure in the mix.

Plan for things to go wrong: Just like you should plan for success, know that everything will not always work as expected. While you have coordinated resources, people, and time to the best of your ability, things will change, and also you have to be open to changing and updating your systems along the way. Adaptability is critical, and this is the learning curve that will help your team get stronger.

Communication, cooperation, and coordination are the 3C's that result in teamwork and collaboration at the highest level.

Your goal should be to keep your eye on these factors at all times. It's also a lot about learning along the way. You will find that your team usually knows more than you do about the work, and that's a good thing. You may also find that bringing various skills together can work wonders for the team, allowing for more cross-pollination of expertise makes the team that much more versatile.

Overall, collaboration is the final piece of the team management puzzle, and it will set your team miles ahead when applied correctly.

6 CONCLUSION - NOW IT'S YOUR TURN

Thank you for taking this fulfilling and exciting journey through team management. There are so many moving parts in a team that it can lead you down many paths.

Your role as a team manager should encompass the vital aspects discussed in this book, including making an adaptive plan, delegating to the right people, establishing a communication model, and finally bring everything together to form a well oiled high performing team through collaboration.

You've learned that failing to plan is planning to fail, so make sure that every step of your team's process and formation gets designed in collaboration with your team. Consider various factors, and seek help where needed but always use planning to understand the objectives of what is required. This step is the building block for getting your team to the final stage of high performance. And it indeed starts by getting to the crux of why your organization exists, looking at the vision, goals, strategy, and challenges associated.

Once you have an adaptive plan, you can quickly move towards addressing delegation within your team. A common question is: "how to delegate effectively?" And that's answered promptly by investigating who will be the right fit for the work you would like to transfer. And this must also consider the person's strengths, current capacity, and more. Once you have a person to delegate to, your work starts by reviewing the steps to game-changing delegation. You will find that the more you delegate, the more empowered your team feels, and the more time you have to focus on various other aspects of your work or business.

Since you've delegated well and had a taste of empowering your team - you can now move forward into mastering the art of communication. You know how important communication can be to getting the job done, as well as to build rapport in your team. Yet, there are many challenges associated, but with simple tools and practical measures, you can conquer all of them.

Think about using technology and direct messaging to your advantage; consider how great managers communicate and use these tools to build those skills. After all, communication skills require training too.

Finally, you have worked through opportunities to get your team on the same page - yet a high performing team needs more work. This work lies in the field of collaboration. Some units can work without cooperation, and they deliver adequate work, yet you should be aiming for superior business outputs that sets your team apart. You do this by following a 5 step framework, including communicating the goals effectively for maximum buy-in, then enhancing cooperation within your organization, and finally coordinating your team's resources and time. These steps will move you to the ultimate teamwork and collaboration.

Team management is not easy; there are many challenges along the way. That said, you have all the tools needed to overcome those challenges and move the needle on your team's performance. These tools will positively impact your company and implicitly make your entire business more productive, efficient, and profitable too.

7 REFERENCES

Corporate Edge. '5 Key Drivers of a High-Performance Team', https://corporate-edge.com.au/ce-author/5-key-drivers-of-a-high-performance-team/

Forbes. 'Your Employee Engagement Strategy Needs More Wellness', https://www.forbes.com/sites/alankohll/2018/07/30/your-employee-engagement-strategy-needs-more-wellness/#4166fa6542b5

Gallup. 'Engagement Keeps the Doctor Away', https://news.gallup.com/businessjournal/14500/engagement-keeps-doctor-away.aspx

Gray Stone Advisors. '7 Ways to Create an Inspiring Team Vision Statement', https://www.graystoneadvisors.com/7-ways-create-inspiring-vision-statement/

Great Place To Work. 'How to Create a Culture of Collaboration in the Workplace', https://www.greatplacetowork.com/resources/blog/how-to-create-a-culture-of-collaboration-in-the-workplace

Growing Leadership. '10 Characteristics of a compelling vision', https://growingleadership.today/10-characteristics-of-a-compelling-vision/

HBR. 'Eight Ways to Build Collaborative Teams', https://hbr.org/2007/11/eight-ways-to-build-collaborative-teams

HubSpot. '17 Truly Inspiring Company Vision and Mission Statement Examples', https://blog.hubspot.com/marketing/inspiring-company-mission-statements

Huffpost. '14 Reasons Why People Cannot or Will Not Delegate Responsibilities', https://www.huffpost.com/entry/14-reasons-why-people-can_b_7945222

LinkedIn. 'Concept of Golden Circle -By Simon Sinek', https://www.linkedin.com/pulse/concept-golden-circle-by-simon-sinek-babak-mohammadi

MindTools. 'Team Management Skills The Core Skills Needed to Manage Your Team', https://www.mindtools.com/pages/article/newTMM_92.htm

Prialto. '7 Leadership Quotes on Delegation to Inspire You to Greatness', https://blog.prialto.com/inspirational-delegation-quotes

Smart Sheet. 'The Basics of Teamwork and Collaboration', https://www.smartsheet.com/collaborative-teamwork

SME Strategy. '4 Keys to Successful Strategic Planning with Your Team', https://www.smestrategy.net/blog/4-keys-to-successful-strategic-planning-with-your-team

Snapcomms. '8 Must Read Employee Engagement Statistics Every Man Manager Should Know', https://www.snapcomms.com/blog/employee-engagement-statistics

Study. 'Delegation in Management: Definition & Explanation', https://study.com/academy/lesson/delegation-in-management-definition-lesson-quiz.html

Tools Hero. ' What is the Simon Sinek Golden Circle? Theory and example?', https://www.toolshero.com/leadership/golden-circle-simon-sinek/

Ux Matters. 'Overcoming Common Barriers to Collaboration, Part 1', https://www.uxmatters.com/mt/archives/2017/10/overcoming-common-barriers-to-collaboration-part-1.php

Wrike. '11 Key Business Benefits of Team Collaboration (& Why You Should Work on Your Teamwork)', https://www.wrike.com/blog/business-benefits-of-team-collaboration/

8 ABOUT THE AUTHORS

Marcel Boer is a solution architect working for one of the largest IT service providers being responsible for conceptualizing, implementing and testing innovative business models.

He is used to managing remote teams and has devoted himself to thought leadership. Leading a team can be exhausting but is inspiring and rewarding.

Emelia Pillay previously managed teams at one of the biggest health insurance companies. She learned many practical aspects of operations management, project management, coaching and leadership fundamentals.

She is currently writing business books, and sharing her experiences being a manager and a leader. It pays to remember that you should lead people, and manage processes.

www.ingramcontent.com/pod-product-compliance
Lightning Source LLC
Chambersburg PA
CBHW050256220526
45465CB00002B/709